HOW TO DEVELOP YOUR PERSONALITY

Courtesy of Mishkin, N. Y.

CLARE TREE MAJOR

HOW TO DEVELOP YOUR PERSONALITY

By

CLARE TREE MAJOR

With a Foreword by

SIR HERBERT TREE

NEW YORK
THOMAS Y. CROWELL COMPANY
PUBLISHERS

For the rights to certain parts of this book, the publisher wishes to acknowledge the courtesy of The McClure Publications, Inc., who published a series of articles by Clare Tree Major on the development of personality.

FOREWORD

BY SIR HERBERT TREE

THE development of personality is a most interesting and vital subject. Not only on the stage, where it is the essential foundation of a career, but in ordinary life, a man's success represents the sum total of his personality.

While it is my opinion that this essential cannot be taught, it can certainly be freed and developed. It is to this end that every department, whether of elocution, of voice production, of dancing, or of pantomime, is planned in the Academy of Dramatic Art of London, of which I was the founder. As a successful graduate of the Academy, Clare Tree Major has based this most interesting work on first hand knowledge of its methods and results.

While it might seem that one system of training, applied to a group of people, would serve to level all to one standard, experience proves that this is not so. At all costs the individuality must be preserved. Such work as that taught at the Academy and advocated in this book modifies, but does not destroy, the imperfections which limit the individuality. Indeed, the physical and vocal responsiveness and control gained, add magnetism and charm to the personality. The suggestions given should prove of great benefit to the readers of this able work.

Herbert B. Tree

PREFACE

BY FRANCIS TREVELYAN MILLER, LITT.D., LL.D.

Founder of "The Journal of American History." Author of "The Portrait Life of Lincoln," Editor-in-chief "Photographic History of the Civil War"

IT seems to me that Clare Tree Major is performing a great service to science and to human prosperity and happiness in teaching us how to discover ourselves.

Throughout the annals of mankind the highest achievements of the human race have depended upon the individual and his ability to express his individuality.

Civilization can rise no higher than the height of its individual members.

If every man and woman would begin today to develop the *best that is in him or her*, we should have a new world of achievement, far greater in the arts and industries than anything heretofore conceived.

The richest mine in the world is the one within yourself—begin today to develop it.

Francis Trevelyan Miller

CONTENTS

PART ONE

PHYSICAL PERSONALITY

PART TWO

VOCAL PERSONALITY

PART ONE

Physical Personality

CHAPTER I

WHAT IS PERSONALITY?

Individuality Is Not Personality—Personality Dependent on Physical, Mental and Emotional Poise—The Fundamentals of Physical Development—The Point of View Toward Development of Personality.

WHAT is "personality"?

Webster interprets the meaning of the word as "individuality," but like many words that assume added meanings through common usage, this also has acquired the suggestion of a quality not covered by the word "individuality." You may be discussing a person you dislike very much, with whose ideas you do not at all agree, who represents a type having a low standard of commercial and social honor, and while you might readily admit that such a person might be "individual," you would never for a moment say "So-and-so has personality." Why? Because the word "personality" has grown to mean magnetic power, the sort of power that consciously or unconsciously dominates and controls the individuals with whom it comes in contact.

It is this magnetic power that is at the root of every successful career.

Review the life of any great man. You will find that his success is the result, not only of careful study and of perseverance, but, more than all, of the subtle influence of personal magnetism. He has succeeded because his personality convinced people that he was sincere, that he was strong, a man on whom they could rely. Without a well-developed personality, his good qualities would have lain unnoticed and he would have been only another in the struggling, discouraged thousands.

Think of the people of your own acquaintance whom you consider successful. When you analyze their characters, you find in each a certain elusive quality that you can't put your finger on and define. That elusive quality is personality. Or, rather, it is personality developed.

If you should ask the director of any school of dramatic art, "What does the instruction given in your institution do for your students?" he would tell you, not that it teaches them to act, to dance, to become elocutionists, but that *it develops personality.*

At the play you sense the wave of response that sweeps through the audience when the star comes on the stage, and you say, "What a magnetic personality!" It is not her beauty, her technic, her knowledge of stage tricks that move you, but her *personality.*

You hear a sermon, a lecture, a speaker at the club. You may not agree with the point of view expressed, but you are influenced against your will by the magnetism of the speaker.

What is this subtle, elusive force, this radiant, vital energy which gives to its fortunate possessor such unlimited possibilities of success in every department of life?

Bliss Carman has said that it is "The balanced perfection of a healthy and beautiful mind, soul, and body." In other words, perfect physical, mental, and emotional poise.

It is on this viewpoint that all educative systems of personal development are based.

As intelligent human beings we demonstrate life in three ways—physically, mentally, and emotionally. It is still an open question, and, because of the impossibility of demonstration, will always remain one to be decided individually, whether we are merely the sum total of these three elements, or whether we are souls, if I may use a much-abused word, having these three channels, through which we contact other souls under the same conditions of physical existence—these three servants which, through their experiences, conduce to our inner growth. This latter idea is by far the most valuable as a starting point for the development of personality; the idea that we are already essentially all our wildest dreams and most aspiring visions would have us be, and that our real task is so to perfect the physical, emotional, and mental channels that they will become free, responsive, eager mediums through which the inexhaustible forces of the primal self may flow in full, spontaneous abundance and power.

The natural point of departure is the physical. You may have wonderful powers of mind and imagination, but if you are physically undeveloped, awkward, out of poise, these powers cannot be expressed with their greatest possibility of strength and beauty.

The magnetic attraction of a sound, healthy physical condition is so well recognized that one writer goes so far as to say that "Magnetism is the result of an abundance of red corpuscles in the blood." That is an exaggeration. This much is true, however: The vitality, the poise, the perfect grace and freedom of every part of the body developed through correct exercise and an intelligent system of life, provide for the inner forces a sympathetic and responsive channel of expression. Nothing is as destructive and cramping to the personality as self-consciousness. The root of self-consciousness lies in an incapability of expression.

If you would be magnetic, be sincere. The incomparable Carlyle, in his lectures on *Hero Worship,* says: "Sincerity, a deep, great, genuine sincerity, is the first characteristic of all men in any way heroic."

Cultivate enthusiastic optimism. Smile. What single attribute wins friends more readily than the sympathetic, responsive, understanding smile?

Don't be afraid to laugh. There is a very real physiological necessity for laughter. The deep, forcible chest movements increase the rapidity of the circulation, securing a more complete oxygenation of the blood, and relieving the brain and nervous system from the strain and tension incident to the affairs of the day.

The consideration of the physical development of personality embraces two divisions, the body and the vocal organs. In the first division we shall take up work for physical health and efficiency, and in the second the fundamentals of voice training, breath control, tone purity, tone placement, articulation, and other phases of vocal beauty.

In each of these departments I shall follow more or less closely the system in use in the Academy of Dramatic Art of London, a system that is the result of patient and intelligent experiment, finally adopted for its proven value in the bringing out of the latent powers of its students.

In selecting the exercises given in Chapter III, which should be performed faithfully every day, preferably just before retiring, I have so arranged them that every part of the body is strengthened and developed. By means of the gradation system, beginning with the more simple ones, and increasing the strain as the muscles become able to respond, we do away with the danger of excess fatigue, and secure a gradual, normal, and healthy development.

But before any effective building-up work can be done, the whole figure must be brought into natural and correct poise.

When the body is properly poised, the weight is carried entirely on the balls of the feet. The heels should not touch the ground except to balance, never to carry the weight. The commonest fault with which the instructor in gymnastics has to deal is the almost universal failing of placing the weight entirely on the heels.

The placing of the weight on the balls of the feet has several distinct effects on the shape and carriage of the body as well as on the condition of the nervous system. With the weight properly placed, the chest is higher, the head erect, the abdomen drawn back, and the spine, with its delicate and sensitive nervous system, drawn into a natural and healthy curve. Figures 1, 2, and 3, illustrated in Chapter III, show examples of incorrect and correct poise. It is impossible to overrate the importance of correct poise. Many cases of nervous disorders are directly due to the irritation and abuse of the nervous organism through constant standing and walking with the weight on the heels, and the consequent incorrect and injurious curvature of the spine.

As an excellent test for faults of poise, stand with heels almost together, and the hands on the hips. Now slowly rise on the toes, carefully noticing just how far you have to sway the body forward before you begin to rise. By just that much you are out of poise. When you are properly poised, you will rise directly to the toes without needing to sway forward. If you find, as you probably will, that your poise is not good, you will gain much benefit from walking about your room, for say three minutes at a time, entirely on the toes, keeping the heels quite free of the floor. The knees should not be stiff, and the walk should be easy and natural. Then try to remember not to let the weight rest on the heels in your ordinary walks and occupations. It is quite difficult at first to correct this injurious habit. It requires persistent watching, but once establish the correction and you have laid a sure and certain foundation for grace and beauty of carriage.

When taking any form of exercise, be sure that no clothing is worn that in any way restricts the movements of the body. Loose blouse and bloomers, or an ordinary combination suit, for women, and trunks for men, is all that should be worn. There should be no heels on the shoes. Indeed, bare or stockinged feet are best.

In examining oneself for physical defects, one should pay close attention to the chest. Round shoulders, sagging chests, hollow necks, and shoulder blades protruding like embryonic wings can all be cured by judicious exercise. The first four exercises in Chapter III are excellent for correcting this condition.

The first thing to establish is an understanding

of your own needs. Don't be afraid to face the worst in yourself. Stand before that good friend that never flatters, your faithful mirror, and try to see yourself as others see you.

Walk, sit, move your hands, your arms, your head, in your habitual way, and judge for yourself as to what needs improvement. Then work to that end. If you are fat and heavy, exercise will reduce you and give you buoyancy and vigor. If you are thin and scrawny, your movements stiff and angular, exercise will fill out the scraggy places and give you grace and freedom of motion.

If you are dull, listless, nervous, suffering from headaches and backaches, exercise, plenty of fresh air and an abundance of pure water will restore your health, give you new life and fill you with vital energy.

Keep firmly in your mind the end you wish to attain. Picture to yourself the glowing complexion, the erect, free, graceful carriage, the symmetry of form, the alert expression, the magnetic vitality of this powerful creature you wish to become. Know that they can all be yours at the expenditure of a little daily, persistent effort, and then work for the fulfilment of your vision. At first the improvement may seem slow. Habits of years are not to be broken in a moment, but soon you will begin to feel a new interest in life, a blessed strength and calmness under nervous strain, and an abounding vigor and energy that will convince you of the value of the discipline you have given yourself. Hope will begin to change to realization and you will know that you are travelling the sure and certain road to the development of a glorious, vital, perfect manhood.

CHAPTER II

RELATION OF BREATHING TO PERSONALITY

Proper Breathing Essential to Health; Health Essential to Personality—How to Use the Lungs Properly—Breathing Through the Skin—Subconscious Control an Element of Development.

GOOD health is the possession of a fine, strong, supple, responsive body; it is a nervous system so keen and controlled that it serves as a perfect medium for the transmission of the electric magnetism which is the very essence of physical and mental vitality. All these are normal and natural conditions that every man may realize if he will but free himself from the habits of thought that prevent their development.

There is no arbitrary law for any man. The laws he benefits or suffers under he makes for himself. All there is of life, of health, of success, of happiness, exists everywhere for everyone. No one man has an option on any portion of the mighty forces that press around us waiting to minister to our need.

But most men have built walls about themselves, walls of depression and discouragement, which reflect physically in lowered vitality and lack of power of resistance; walls of fear and self-distrust, that vitiate their efforts before they are materialized. Behind these walls they hide, all so unconsciously, and never dream that flowing around them are the great waves of the mighty sea of universal power, if they would but break down the walls that confine them and trust themselves to it.

To them I would say, "Come out, out into the freedom of the glorious sunshine, yes, even out into the freedom of the great storms, and realize the full strength of your manhood—your manhood that is in its essence Godhood."

Your first freedom can be realized physically. Stop thinking that you are getting old, that your joints are stiff, that you inherited something that limits you. You are your own limitation. Begin to exercise and realize your physical freedom, and learn from that that all other freedom is yours for the taking.

In the previous chapter I have laid some stress on the need of building up the chest. Certainly nothing lends more grace and dignity to the whole bearing than the well-developed chest and erect, delicately poised head. There are much more important reasons, however, than this that the chest should be well cared for. The evils attendant on a weak and relaxed condition of the chest are innumerable. Most important is the effect on the lungs.

Perfect health without proper breathing is a physical impossibility. This is easy to understand if you remember that one-third of the entire volume of blood is always circulating in the lungs. Each corpuscle passes through the lungs eight thousand times in twenty-four hours. These little soldiers of the blood come hurrying up, bringing their load of poisonous carbonic acid to be disposed of in the lungs, and then hurry back to the tissues with the life-giving oxygen they have taken from the air forced into the lungs by the breath. When the breathing is shallow, or the air impure, the little messengers must carry away part of the poison they brought with them, and not only is the physical system weakened, but these valuable little disease destroyers are themselves starved for lack of proper nourishment. Deep, full respiration is the quickest and best cure for anemia, or thinness of the blood, and nervousness.

In my experience as a teacher, covering a number of years, with pupils of all ages, I have been surprised at the widespread ignorance of what deep breathing really means. My first instruction to a new pupil is, "Take a strong, deep breath." Almost invariably I am rewarded by a tremendous puffing up of the upper chest, with the consequent restriction of the lower lungs and a total immovability of the diaphragm. It seems to me that a very slight knowledge of anatomy should be sufficient to prevent such an absurd misconception of terms. It is as though one should tell a man to dig a deep hole in the ground, and he should immediately climb a tree.

The great mass of the lungs is situated directly

under the ribs, and the point of greatest distension is just above the waist-line. There is nothing in the chest to inflate but two small points that can be distinctly felt if the hand is firmly pressed on them during inhalation. These should be inflated, of course, but if the chest is built high by exercise, the pressure of air from the lower lungs will force itself into the upper without effort. Fill the lower lungs and the rest will take care of itself.

In the exercises given in Chapter III, I have included one for the increase and control of the breath supply. I have done this, however, merely to initiate an interest in this most important subject, and your practice of deep breathing should be by no means confined to this simple exercise.

The value of fresh air, air that has been vivified and electrified through the action of the rays of the sun, has been thoroughly demonstrated during the last few years. It is hard to appreciate the mental attitude of people of even the last decade, who would shut up an ailing patient in a closed room, and feel that anyone opening the window would be attempting the murder of the unfortunate sick. Now that we keep sufferers from tuberculosis strictly out of doors, now that hospital windows are seldom closed, now that almost all new houses are built with sleeping porches as a matter of course, now that the medical fraternity and the layman are alike educated to the value of an abundant supply of clean, pure air, is it not an astonishing thing that so few people make any effort to utilize or benefit by this generous gift?

The widespread ignorance of correct methods of breathing, and of the injurious consequences of such inability, is appalling, and yet surely it requires but a little common sense and practical experiment to set one right in this respect. First find out the size and elasticity of your lungs by experimentation. Place your hands on your chest and concentrate all your breath in the upper part of your lungs. You will feel the pressure under your hands, particularly if you are careful to keep the shoulders from rising. Now place your hands on either side of your body, just above the waist-line, and concentrate all your breath there. That will acquaint you with the greater bulk of your lung mass. Now place the hands on the back, with the thumbs to the front, and concentrate all your breath force in the back part of your lungs. Under four finger-tips you will feel the lungs contract and expand, completing your education regarding the size and position of these, the most important organs of the human body.

In this way we have learned that common sense requires that we fill the lungs at their greatest thickness, which is under the three lower ribs, and by concentrating strongly on this part, the overflow will press itself up into the smaller part.

Now let us apply the same test to the method of exhaling. In this regard we have three agencies to reckon with: the natural elasticity of the lungs, the relaxation of the ribs, and the relaxation of the diaphragm. While in anything like an entire evacuation of the lungs of all air a combination of these three elements would be employed, the actual breath control should center in the diaphragm. The first expansion on inhalation takes place at the waist-line and continues up into the chest region; similarly, the first relaxation takes place in the diaphragm, and is continued by the relaxation of the lower ribs. Further than this, however, the relaxation should not go, as the chest should not at any time fall, and at no time during inhalation should it appreciably rise. You may possibly disagree with me on this, but try it for yourself. When you take a chest breath and raise your shoulders, what has happened to your ribs and that most important muscle, the diaphragm? The diaphragm has been muscularly drawn up, so that as an expelling medium its power is destroyed, and the ribs also have been drawn together, squeezing all the air out of the largest and most elastic portion. Common sense again, you see, is our teacher.

Do not confine your indulgence in fresh air to the inside of your body. Your skin also needs to breathe. It is unfortunate that the chemical action of the skin as a health preserver is so little understood. Many people who take daily baths from habit do not at all realize the reason for the comfort they feel. Much hard work can be saved the kidneys by keeping the skin in an active, healthy condition, since through its millions of sudorific glands the skin can eliminate many of the toxic elements that would otherwise pass through the kidneys. Plenty of water and fresh air for the skin are as important as for the interior of the body. For some period during the day, even if only for ten or fifteen minutes, all clothing should be removed and the air and sunlight be allowed free play over the nude body. Indeed, on every occasion when practicable, either in one's own room with the windows wide open, or in any out-door space that can be protected from overlooking, partial or entire nudity should be followed. The importance of proper ventilation and elimination through the skin is shown in the fact that the entire varnishing of the body is followed invariably by most serious effects, sometimes by death.

One important thing to remember in all methods of physical training is the absolute obedience given by the body to the mind that inhabits it. So much has been written about the subconscious mind, and so much of the writing is so intolerably dry, that many people instinctively shrink from reading anything in which the word occurs. There is such sound reasoning at the base of the theory, however, that we must take it into account in our endeavor to bring out this inner something which marks us "ourselves." Certainly our muscles have no power of themselves to change. You may put an intoxicated man through all the exercises that have ever been invented, and you would obtain no change in his muscular condition. The exercises do but one thing, and their success depends entirely on the extent to which you concentrate on that one thing. It is just this: they call the attention of the active or positive thought to the change which you as an individual desire to take place in those muscles that you are at the moment exercising. That is why I say to you, "Have in your mind a definite picture of what you wish to become." An artist does not try to paint a great picture without models on which he bases his conception of the ideal. Neither should you begin your physical training without a very definite picture in your mind which you will train your body to imitate or become. Cultivate an admiration for health, and poise, and physical beauty. When you walk on the street, watch with pleasure the people you meet who demonstrate in themselves the conditions you wish to possess. Encourage your body by dwelling on every improvement, no matter how small, that you make from day to day. I have always found that pupils who approach their work from this standpoint get much greater and more permanent results than those who distrust themselves and do the exercises simply because they are told to do so.

Even those most discouragingly practical people, medical scientists, are beginning to agree that the body is made up of millions of tiny atoms that seem to have a separate and individual intelligence of their own apart from their mass intelligence as a body. Whether this mass consciousness is to be credited with the improvement brought about through exercise, by attracting through the mind force employed an added number of units to the muscles under exercise; or whether in some specific region of the brain there is an action that we are not conscious of when the mind is occupied with external things, and that this action continues the work set it at intervals by the active mind; at least one thing is certain, that we are physically what we think or expect ourselves to be. The more we invest our physical training with the confidence of hope and expectation, the more rapidly and surely are those hopes and expectations materialized and realized.

When you have completed the graded course of exercise arranged in the next chapter, work out for yourself a system of exercise compiled from the last of the three months that will take care of your specific needs, and then faithfully perform them each morning on arising or at night on retiring, as a constitutional part of your toilet. Persistence is essential if you would keep yourself up to the standard of magnetic virility which is in itself a road to all attainments, a standard which does not know the words "despondency" and "depression," and which makes the hardest fight only one more opportunity for the glory of conquest, the greatest obstacles but the medium through which you may feel the crowning joy of the conqueror.

CHAPTER III

GRADED EXERCISES

Specially Graded System of Exercises for the Development of Physical Health, Symmetry and Poise—Outlined for First, Second and Third Months.

THERE is no greater misnomer in the English language than that exemplified by the rare faculty we term "common sense." Notwithstanding its uncommonness, however, we must presuppose its possession by everybody who aspires to the cultivation of the power of personal magnetism.

Perhaps in no other division of our task shall we need common sense more than in connection with physical development. It is in accordance with its dictates that we arrange our exercise in graded sequence, beginning with simple corrective work, and gradually leading up to the more difficult and strenuous. One must use one's reason, too, with regard to persistence and regularity. More harm than good may be done by spasmodic periods of vigorous exercise interspersed with periods of muscular idleness. Ten or fifteen minutes of faithful work every day will give much better and more permanent results than will working half an hour a day for a week and then allowing the exercises to cease for three or four days.

Be very careful that you thoroughly understand

the exercises before putting them into practice. Compare your movements with the text as you work out the instructions, and do not repeat as an exercise until you are certain you are correct.

To test Exercise 1, stand with the right side a few inches from the wall. If you are getting the best results possible from this exercise, the tips of the fingers will trace on the wall a large circle of which the shoulder is the center. The body should not change its position when the arm is forming the back of the circle.

You will notice that a great number of the exercises are given for the back. Modern methods of dress, and our unnatural habits of living, especially the sedentary habits of the city dweller, have resulted in great general deterioration of the important muscles and extensors of the back. Exercise 17, which should not be attempted until it occurs in its regular graded position, is particularly valuable in this connection.

This whole exercise may be entirely impossible at the first attempt. The weight of the feet will seem too great to lift, and when you have succeeded in raising them, to lower them slowly will seem impossible. Every muscle, from the scalp to the thighs, will seem almost at breaking point. A little perseverance and persistence will soon overcome these unpleasant sensations, and every muscle, especially of the back and abdomen, will be immensely benefited.

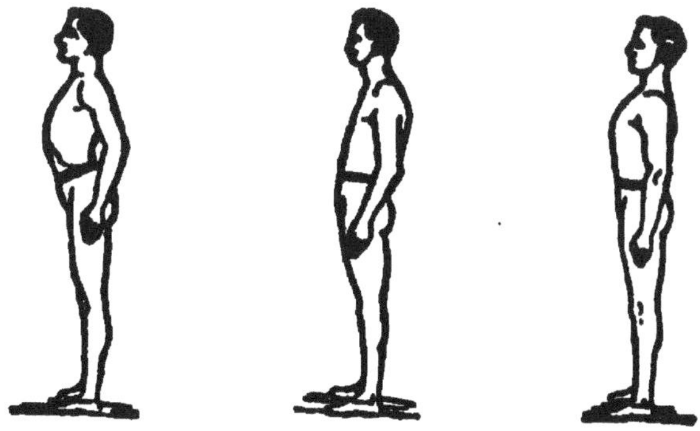

Incorrect Incorrect Correct

Figures 1, 2 and 3

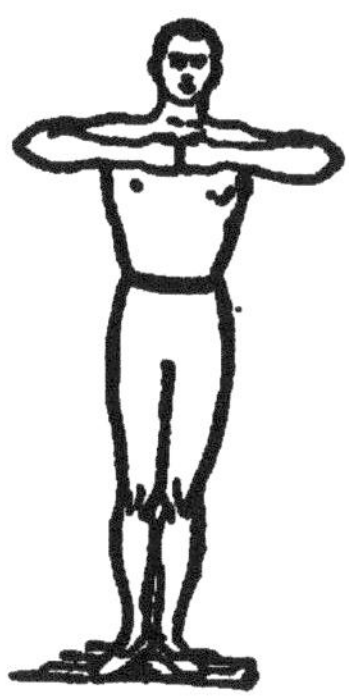

Figure 4

Illustrating Exercise 3
First Month, Chapter III

Figure 5

Illustrating Exercise 4
First Month, Chapter III

Figure 6

Illustrating Exercise 5
First Month, Chapter III

Correct Incorrect

Figures 7 and 8

Illustrating Exercise 6
First Month, Chapter III

Figure 10

Illustrating Exercise 14
Second Month, Chapter III

Illustrating Exercise 13
Second Month, Chapter III

Figure 9

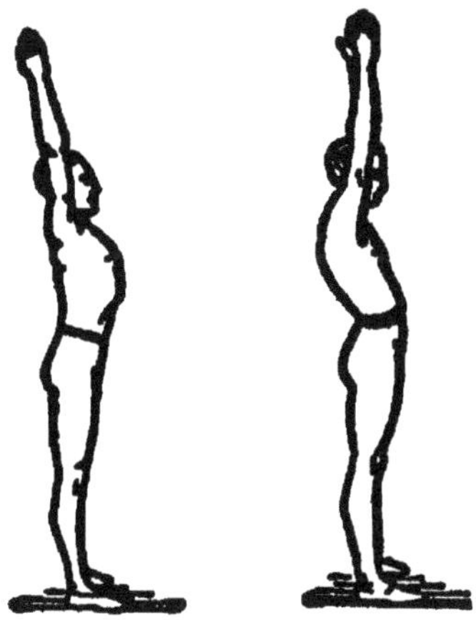

Correct Incorrect

Figures 11 and 12

The Correct and Incorrect Methods
of Raising the Arms.
See Chapter VII, page 81.

clasped behind. Turn the hands so that the palms are toward the back, with the elbows straightened. Now bend forward, and raise the clasped hands as high as possible. Bend backward, pushing the clasped hands as far down the legs as possible. Repeat five times.

This is an excellent exercise for flattening protruding shoulder-blades.

13. For trunk and waist—Stand with the feet apart and arms slightly relaxed, extended above head. Bend to the right, directly over right hip, then to the left, five times each. (See Figure 9.)

14. For the spine and abdomen—Stand erect, with hands above head. Rise upon the toes, then sink the body to the floor, bending the knees sharply, and pressing them to the right and left as far as possible, keeping the weight well on the toes. The trunk must be kept erect. As you sink to the floor, draw the arms down so that they are extended at the sides, as in Figure 10. Repeat five times. This squatting exercise is an excellent one for reducing a fleshy abdomen, as well as strengthening the muscles.

THIRD MONTH

Cease Exercises 7 and 9, and reduce Exercise 6 to three times. Reduce Exercise 11 to five times.

Add

15. For the muscles of the back—Lie on the floor on your back, with arms folded across chest.

Slowly raise the body to a sitting posture without letting the heels leave the floor. Slowly lower body to original position. Three times is a sufficient number to begin with. If necessary, the feet can be slipped under the bar of a chair for the first few times until the muscles are strong enough to support the weight alone.

16. Kneel on the left knee, with the face forward, and the right arm held straight up by the side of the head. The left hand rests on the hip. Now turn the entire trunk and head slowly to the left as far as possible. Slowly return to original position. Repeat five times. Change to right knee, extend left arm, and repeat the exercise to the right.

17. Lie on your back on the floor, and fold your arms across your chest. Now with as little bend at the knees as possible, and keeping the feet slightly apart, raise your legs slowly until they are at right angles with your body, extending straight upward. Now lower them slowly to the ground again, seeing to it that the head does not rise from its position on the floor. Repeat but once or twice at the first trial, increasing to five times as the muscles strengthen.

18. Fold your arms across your back, clasping each elbow with the opposite hand. Now kneel on the right knee very slowly, and as soon as the right knee touches the floor, immediately begin to rise again very slowly. This exercise is only valuable if performed very slowly. Once for each knee to

begin, increasing to three for each knee as muscles strengthen.

19. Relaxing exercise to finish all exercise periods. Stand with the feet slightly apart, and the weight well on the toes. Let the head fall forward on the chest in an absolutely relaxed condition, so that it feels as though it were tied on with a string. Now let the shoulders sag forward, and begin to bend, letting the dead feeling creep down the spine until the upper part of the body is bending forward, literally hanging at the waist-line. The legs and hips must remain energized rather strongly or you will lose your balance. Now begin to rise by allowing the life to creep back up along the spine, keeping the arms, shoulders and head relaxed to the very end, when they energize in their natural order. Finish the upward movement by clenching the hands, raising the chest to its highest point, and taking a deep, strong inhalation. This exercise is very refreshing and restful to the nervous system.

PART TWO

Vocal Personality

CHAPTER IV

THE PERSONALITY OF THE VOICE

The Practical Value of the Voice—How to Cure a Grouch—Use of the Voice in Business—Fundamentals of Voice Culture.

ONE of the greatest and most potent charms possible to possess is that of a beautiful, well-modulated, sympathetic voice. In public life, in society, in the office, the workshop, and in the home it proves itself an important factor to success. A man's voice not only indicates his character, but by reaction on his mind helps to form that character. Do you get full, rich, round tones from the man who is down and out? Neither does the man of action, of quick, decisive thought, speak in a whining, hesitating voice. The man who knows he is a failure speaks in an apologetic whine. The very sound that betrays him as a failure reacts on himself and on others and helps to make him one. One may lie with words, but it is very hard to lie with one's voice. It is responsive to shades of thought that are almost unconscious, and if an effort is made to control its indication of feeling, it will expose the hypocrisy by the shallow, hard, insincere quality of its tones.

The unconsciously employed tones of the voice

not only indicate one's mood, but can be used, by force of reaction, to change one's mood. Try it some time when you are feeling blue and depressed. Take some stirring passage: Shakespeare's Henry V. speech to his soldiers, beginning, "Once more unto the breach, dear friends," or some of the martial speeches from Scott's *Marmion and Douglas*. Forget the trouble that brought on the depressing mood. Take a deep breath that fills every cell of your lungs, and then read aloud with all the fervor of which you are capable. Picture yourself in King Henry's place, with the breach already made in the walls, and the success of the battle depending on these good British soldiers waiting his word to renew the attack. It is a hand-to-hand conflict that must be fought by inspiration. See that you inspire them. When you come to the close of the speech you will have forgotten that you were depressed. The trouble will have dwindled in proportion to the rise of your courage, induced by employing words and tones suggesting the successful fight and fighter.

If one's voice can react on oneself in this way, how much must it mean to others, who either consciously or unconsciously base their judgment of one on the effect they feel from one's voice. One cannot imagine Mr. Roosevelt with a small, colorless voice. It would not indicate the type of man. Mr. Bryan's success as a speaker is due to the particular quality of his voice.

There is a language of the voice apart altogether

from the use of words. Try it with some simple selection. Read it joyfully, read it sadly, read it triumphantly, read it with exaltation, then notice how your own feeling answers to the sound of your voice, even though the words may carry no particular meaning to your mind.

In this way you will learn what a powerful, responsive servant the well-trained voice may be. There is no reason at all why the business man should not train and use his voice with as deliberate control and as good effect as is shown by the greatest artists of the theater. On the stage the psychology of the voice is understood and used with deliberate effect. If you think over the comparatively few great actresses who have made international reputations for themselves, you will find that in each case the medium through which they have moved their audiences to tears and laughter, to indignation and sorrow, to every emotion the human heart is capable of feeling, has been the responsive, controlled, cultivated voice.

It is said of Mrs. Siddons, the greatest actress of her day, that even in her old age she could sit in her drawing-room and read Shakespeare so wonderfully that those who heard her lost all sense of time and place, and saw the drama realistically unfolding itself before their eyes.

In our own day, how many of the millions who have flocked to hear Sarah Bernhardt have entirely understood the spoken words of the drama? But the haunting tones of her marvelous voice speak a language to the heart that does not need the interpretation of words. Love, anger, hatred, fear, pity, sorrow, despair—every sound is vibrant with its own emotion. To think of Peter Pan is to hear Maude Adams's voice. To read a play embodying some lofty idea, some absorbing passion of the human soul, is to long to hear it made alive through the compelling magnetism of Edith Wynne Matthison's exquisite voice. Julia Marlowe was Juliet because she had Juliet's voice. And so we might go on, always finding that the greatest actress is no greater than her voice.

It is a great mistake to think either that one cannot change one's method of speech, or that the result, should one do so, would be unnatural or insincere. Nothing that is correct, and beautiful because it is correct, or inversely, can be unnatural. If you had grown up in a locality where the grammar was poor and you discovered that your method of speaking was incorrect, you would immediately change to the correct method. Why not, then, with the voice as well?

First of all, as with everything else, one must set a standard, a mental picture of the qualities one wishes to develop. The elements that enter into the character of the voice are few and simple. The first is the supply and control of the breath. Second, the absolute relaxation of the vocal cords and throat muscles. Next, the placing of the tone, which for the speaking voice is always well forward toward the lips. Then, the efficiency of lips, teeth and tongue for clear and accurate articulation. Last, but by no means least, tone color, suggested by the emotions, but unconsciously produced by the resonators. Inflection also is an element of interpretation, but is really the use of varying pitches of the fundamental sound after it is produced, not a character of the sound itself.

In discussing the various methods of the development of vocal beauty and purity, I shall deal entirely with the voice in its relation to speech. To those of my readers who are interested in the development of the singing voice, I would repeat the words of Pacchierotti, the greatest singer of the eighteenth century: "He who knows how to speak and breathe knows how to sing." Whatever faults or inefficiencies you may be working against in your singing studies, you will find have their foundation in an incorrect use of the speaking voice, and can be most easily and permanently corrected from that basis.

An increase and control of the breath supply is the normal beginning of any system of voice culture. You may go through all the movements necessary to produce the most exquisite music on a perfect organ, but if you have neglected to pump air into the reeds, you will get no sound. If the air supply is weak and insufficient, the sound, as the result, is squeaky and spasmodic. The quality of the instrument is not at fault, but before it can show you its quality it must be supplied with a sufficient amount of air under the proper degree of compression. This is exactly true of the voice. Full, rich, resonant tone quality depends absolutely on the capacity of the lungs, the great air reservoirs of the body, and the ability to control their action.

In order to breathe well one must learn to stand well. The chest must be carried high and it and the ribs must be well expanded. The waist-line, the region of the diaphragm, must be free and unrestricted and the abdomen drawn back in its proper place. All this can be accomplished by following the suggestions regarding physical training in the department for physical development immediately preceding this.

Having learned fully to inflate every part of the lungs, and not only, as is so often the case, the small part that runs up into the chest, the next step is to establish diaphragmatic control.

As we have already learned in our health breathing, three elements enter into the control of the breath, and consequently into the control of the voice. First, the natural elasticity of the lungs, which have the same tendency automatically to expel the air that an inflated toy balloon would have; second, the relaxation of the muscles of the ribs; third, the most important, the relaxation of the diaphragm.

The chest should never be allowed to move. As

well put one's foot on a hose and expect to obtain a full, strong stream of water, as to attempt to produce a full, rich tone through a relaxed chest.

A test of the correct method of breath control is easily made. Inhale strongly through the nostrils until the lungs are felt pushing firmly against the ribs and waist-line. *Remember that the chest must not rise.* The greatest expansion must be just above the waist-line, where the greatest mass of the lungs is located. Now begin to blow, as you would blow out a match, but with a soft, slow, even pressure, taking as long as possible to completely expel the breath. As you blow, the first relaxation should be that of the diaphragm, the large muscle just below the waist-line. If you push the ribs well outward while expelling the breath, the diaphragm will be felt relaxing and lifting itself upward. The next movement is the relaxation of the ribs, and finally, in complete exhalation, the relaxation of the chest. Used as an exercise for five minutes every day, this is one of the best possible means of establishing correct control of the breath for health as well as vocal purposes. It will also maintain the elasticity of the intercostal muscles, since the ultimate aim will be to keep the ribs as well as the chest always expanded in order to preserve a reserve force of breath at all times.

Another excellent method of increasing the supply and control of the breath is to choose some certain speech and read it aloud each day, increasing each time as far as possible the number of words spoken in one breath.

Still another excellent method is that of progressive counting. Place your hands on either side of your body just above the waist-line so that you can sense whether or not you are concentrating your breathing in the right place. Inhale to your fullest capacity, and, with a strong drawing in of the diaphragm as you speak, count 1. If you are doing it in the right way, the sound will be sharply explosive. Do not exhale the remaining breath, but fill up with a quick inhalation through the mouth, and count, in the same way, 1, 2. Again fill up your breath loss, and count 1, 2, 3. Inhale, count 1, 2, 3, 4. Continue in this way up to 10 to begin with, increasing to 15 in a few weeks, and eventually increasing to 20. It is important that there be no exhalation except that unconsciously occurring in the use of the voice in counting. The only time to inhale is after the highest number in each count, never between. Count slowly and distinctly. When you can count from one to twenty progressively in this way without discomfort, you will have secured a breath supply and control sufficient for any purpose for which you may need it, whether in speaking or singing.

Elementary sound is produced by the flowing of the breath over the vocal cords in much the same way that sound is produced by the passage of air under compression through an organ reed.

In his excellent work on practical phonology,

The Voice, Professor Aikin says of this comparison: "The air pumped into the wind chest is trying to escape—that is, it is under compression. Its only outlet is through the narrow slit at the free edges of an elastic plate, forming what is known as a vibrator or 'reed.' The force of the escape causes this to oscillate in such a manner that its fine slit is repeatedly opened and closed, and the air passes out in a rapid succession of minute puffs, and transmits to the surrounding air a regular series of undulations or sound waves of the same frequency."

From this description the relation of the human voice to the organ is easy to trace. The lungs may be compared to the wind chest of the organ. At the top of the windpipe, through which the breath must pass in order to reach the outer air, are placed the vocal cords. These two membranes, which are exceedingly elastic, are firmly fastened at the sides, but have their center edges free. It is the rapid vibration of these free edges through the passage of the breath that produces sound.

Having pumped the air into our organ, our next concern is with the quality of the sound it is going to produce.

CHAPTER V

THE QUALITY OF THE VOICE

A Common Fault and Its Remedy—The Correct Production of Sound—The Importance of the Vowels—Consonants and Their Relation to Euphonious Diction.

THE fundamental sound of the human voice is "Ah." This is the pure sound, the only sound that can be produced when the mouth is naturally opened, the tongue resting in a relaxed condition in the floor of the mouth, with its tip lightly touching the lower front teeth, and the throat muscles and vocal cords also perfectly relaxed. All other sounds require the deliberate and intentional use of some one or other combination of several organs of articulation.

This, then, is the logical point of commencement for our vocal work. The musical quality of the tone will be governed by the size and shape of the resonators, the hollow spaces in the neck, nose and mouth, which naturally differ in each individual. They can, however, be enlarged and shaped by training, so that the sound may become fuller and more tonal.

It is unnecessary here to enter into any more technical description of the resonator. Its use is to reinforce and enrich the voice, literally to "re-sound," and our effort in connection with it must be toward keeping the passages clear and unrestricted.

One of the most common and injurious faults is that of tightening the muscles before vowel sounds so that they are preceded by the sound and sensation of a slight cough. Suppose we experiment with the letter "A" pronounced as in "face." Repeat it slowly, at first softly, but increase in tone with every repetition. If there is the slightest sensation in the throat of muscular effort, you are using your voice incorrectly. You may not notice the physical sensation perhaps, through familiarity, but if you listen you will discover that the sound begins with a sharp effect, which I can describe in no other way than that already given, as a very slight cough. This is called a glottic shock, and is not only injurious to the vocal organs themselves, but entirely destroys the emotional power of the voice.

To remedy this, practice the vowel sounds in this way: Open the mouth so that the teeth are about an inch apart. (If you have any difficulty in preserving this distance, place a little prop or part of a match between the teeth on either side.) Let the tip of the tongue rest lightly against the lower teeth, the body of the tongue lying flat and relaxed in the floor of the mouth. Begin with the sound "A" as in "father." Let the throat muscles be absolutely relaxed and obtain your pressure by drawing in the diaphragm.

It is sometimes helpful to place the letter "Y" before the vowel if the habit is found very difficult of correction. This merely involves raising the tongue a little in the center. As you begin to succeed in using the diaphragm as a source of power instead of the throat muscles, you can gradually lessen the "Y" sound, until at last you can produce the sound "Ah" without shock and without the assistance of the "Y."

When you have succeeded in obtaining a full, open tone on this, go on with the other open vowel sounds in the following order:

a	u	er	a	e	eh	i	ee
Bard	Bud	Bird	Bat	Bed	Bait	Bit	Beet

You will notice that the body of the tongue rises a little with each sound, so that on "ee" the tongue is at its highest point. The tip of the tongue must remain in its original position, just touching the lower teeth. Work on these until you can repeat them in either direction with perfect freedom from muscular constriction and with full diaphragmatic control. You will then have mastered one of the most vital fundamental principles of vocal beauty.

In addition to these vowels, which are all derived from the fundamental sound "Ah," modified by the rising of the tongue, there are four vowels derived from the same fundamental sound, but modified by the shape of the lips. These are OO, Oh, Aw, O (as in "not"). For OO (as in "pool") the lips are entirely round, pursed up into the smallest compass. Open the lips a little way, and you have the oval shape for "O." Open them a little further and you have "Aw." Open them still further and you have "O" (as in "not"). Open them yet a little wider at the sides and you are back again at the starting point, "Ah."

All these are simple sounds. There are also the compound vowels, used in such words as Duke, Bough and Oil. The "U" in Duke is a combination of "I" (as in "hit,") and "OO." The "ou" in Bough is a combination of "Ah" and "OO," so that it would be pronounced almost as "Bahoo." The sound in Oil is a combination of "aw" and "i" (as in "hit").

All this may sound very uninteresting and possibly unnecessary until one begins to experiment with one's individual pronunciation. All the music, the beauty, the emotion of a language is in the vowel sounds. The consonants merely control the shape of the word. Its character is given by the vowel. A useful little simile is to suppose that the vowels are primal liquid sounds, and the consonants the molds or forms into which this liquid sound is poured in order to divide it off and form it into words. Now you see how essential it is that the vowels shall be pure in quality, neither reflecting any quality that should properly belong to another, and that the articulation of the consonants, that governs the shape of the word, should be clean and true.

Notice the effect on the compound vowel "ow," for instance, when it is properly produced. In many parts of the United States it is given almost the sound of ah, the word *cow* sounding almost like *cah.* In other sections of the country it has a sound of *keoew.* Both types of sound are produced in the back part of the mouth. The correct pronunciation, as we have seen, is a combination of ah-oo, produced right at the lips, as cah-oo. The resonance is tremendously increased and the word becomes musical and agreeable.

There is always a very real and scientific physiological as well as phonological reason for any arbitrary standard of sound. Still using the word "cow," notice how much fuller and rounder the tone "ah-oo" is than any modification that occurs in localism of pronunciation. This is brought about by the increase in size and the improved shape of the resonators when the sound is given as "ah-oo." This result is also assisted by the necessity of the entire rounding of the lips in order to produce the pure sound "oo."

You will add, then, to your practice of the vowels modified by the tongue, these that are modified by the shape of the lips:

oo	oh	aw	o
Boot	boat	law	Bob

As before, you will not say the words; you will use only the vowel sound.

Be careful, as with the others, that there is no glottic shock, or little cough before the emission of the first sound, and then let the breath flow right on through the series.

Remember always that there must be no constriction of the throat muscles. The resonators *must* be relaxed and open. Many teachers advocate the practice of yawning before practicing vowel sounds, in order to show the student the position the tongue and throat should take for the perfect passage of a full open tone.

You have learned now to increase the breath supply, and to control its use by the action of the diaphragm. You have purified the vowel sounds and made them full, round and musical. You have learned to relax the throat so that you are no longer conscious of effort in its muscles when you wish to speak.

Our next task is with the consonants, to make them clear and definite. Remember they are to form the molds into which we are to pour the beautiful sounds we have learned to make, in order to shape and modify them into language.

When the consonants are neglected the speech is careless and slovenly. If they are over-emphasized it is stilted and affected.

The most sinned against of all the letters of the alphabet are the explosives, P, B, T and D, with final L running them a close second. The muscles of the lips may be trained and strengthened by the following practice: Close the lips firmly together, and open them suddenly on the " P " position without the sound of the letter, so that you get a sort of popping effect. No breath must be allowed to escape. When you can do this, add the letter " a," *ap*, and practice it in semitones from G to C, always giving the final " P " the explosive quality. Follow the same system with " T," pressing the tip of the tongue firmly against the hard palate, the roof of the mouth just behind the front teeth, and bringing it away sharply with an explosive sound. Add " a " —*at*, and practice with semitones, as with *ap*. Practice the letter " L " in order to give flexibility to the tip of the tongue.

The use of the letter M is valuable in that it helps to bring the tone forward to the lips. In speech the sounds should flow freely from the lips, and great care should be taken in the foregoing exercises that the tone placement is well forward.

This last is so important that one might almost say that any sound that forces the tone back is incorrect. Think for a moment, in this connection, of our various methods of pronouncing the letter " R." In the West it is formed entirely with the center of the tongue, so that abroad we are accused of saying " Amurica " instead of America. In the South we get no final " R " at all, only an exaggerated " u " sound. The letter " R " when used in the body of the word should be pronounced quite at the tip of the tongue, there being no difference in the sound of the " me " in " America " and the " me " in " met." Taking the same position of the tongue as for " met," you trill the " r " and you have the correct sound. See again how much more musical and resonant the correct sound is than the incorrect.

One should listen to one's voice and try to discover its faults, then work to rectify them. There is no more excuse for going through life with a thin, flat, monotonous voice than with an ugly, undeveloped body.

True, we cannot all have such exquisite voices as Miss Edith Wynne Matthison's, for instance. Such voices have something inborn in them that cannot be imparted to others, but at least they can serve as examples of vocal beauty that should serve to raise our standard, and encourage a more general appreciation of the value of the music that lies in the spoken word. At least every voice can be freed of technical imperfections, improved in tone quality, developed in roundness, depth and purity, and made a fit and responsive medium of expression for every thought and emotion of the individual mind.

CHAPTER VI

WHAT THE VOICE BETRAYS

National Standards of Speech—Flagrant Abuses—How to Change a Nasal Voice—A Man Is Known by His Voice—The Charm of Inflection.

THE American nation is unique in many ways. Every American is justly proud of his birth, because of the things the nation represents among the peoples of the world. Her natural resources are so tremendous that their possession in the hands of one single race is unequaled in the annals of history. Toward the formation of her people as a race the cream of all European nations has contributed. The dangers and privations of the early days, the horrors of internal war, freedom from the restraint of class and tradition, these and other elements have made a people strong, independent, warm-hearted and clear-minded; a people of indomitable courage, where no man's conviction is another man's law; where every man's worth is his own worth; where the shoeblack may yet, if he has it in him, rise to presidency of the people.

American ambition, however, which seeks to be first in commerce, first in invention, first in all legitimate fields of development, is no longer content to take the hindmost place in personal culture. Heretofore America has been unique in this respect also, that among all the civilized nations, she alone had no standard of speech. Proud of the fact that you could not keep a good man down in America, the speech and manners of a veritable boor have been excused because the boor was fortunate enough to make a big fortune in real estate or by some lucky chance owned a well in an oil boom.

This condition, which is so unworthy of the American people, is now most certainly on the wane. America is beginning to demand, not that the man who is fortunate enough to make money should be kept out of the society of the more educated because of his method of speech, or that he should be subjected to the indignity and humiliation incident to his recognizing the difference between his method and theirs, but that every child should be taught and each adult should acquire such a standard of speech that this condition could not arise.

It is as easy to teach the child good English as bad. He can learn only what he hears. Generally speaking, you can rate a man's birth and social position, in almost any other country, by his speech. This is an injustice to the man. America must set her standard of purity of speech and maintain it so that every child, no matter what his station in life, knows but the one system of language, the perfect one. It is here that the responsibility of the parents and teachers comes in. Unless they first work to set the example, the child is helpless.

There are some faults we can correct without the help of a teacher. One of them is the habit of dropping the final consonants. " Ing," for instance, is one flagrant example of this nature. How often one hears it: " I'm goin' downtown "; " I was comin' home "; " I was sittin' there," and so on, *ad lib.* Surely this is unforgivable. If you find this is one of your faults, write out a list of words ending in " ing," and read them faithfully each day until your ear has grown accustomed to the correct sound, when you will no longer offend in this way.

This is also an excellent way to cure such faults of pronunciation as substituting " awn " for " on." Write out your list of words, every one you can think of embodying this sound, and then read it aloud each day. " On," " along," " Boston," not " awn," " alawng," " Bawston."

An important factor in the quality of tone is the pitch at which the voice is habitually used. Most voices are pitched too high, and since the tendency is to raise the pitch under excitement or nervous strain, sharp, hard tones result which are not only disagreeable for others to listen to, but which react as an irritant on the nervous system of the unfortunate possessor. The normal range of the voice is two octaves, and the pitch of the speaking voice should be about the central tone. You can find this for yourself by trying your range with the piano. If you cannot be quite certain, take the lower tone in preference to the higher.

The term "nasal tone," so commonly used to describe a certain quality of voice, is entirely erroneous. The nasal passages form a most important part of the resonance chamber, and no pure tone can be produced without their aid. What is commonly termed a "nasal tone" is caused by the passages of the nose being partially closed, and an incorrect, backward placement of the tone. The size and shape of the resonator differs so largely in individuals that it would be impossible to give detailed instruction practical to follow without a teacher. But this much each one can do for herself: Keep the nasal passages clear and open. Train the mouth to instinctively adopt the correct shape for each sound. See that the back of the tongue is kept well down when practicing, so that the throat spaces are made as large as possible.

In all our work so far we have been dealing with the fundamentals of sound production and its control as language. But there is a value of speech that lies in a quality altogether apart from the mere mechanics of sound, perfect diction, correct grammar and so on. Its real value lies in the use of good diction and articulation through which to pour the other quality, the expression through emphasis, inflection, and tone of color of the finest and most delicate shades of the thought that first must inspire the speech.

Emphasis is the laying of special stress on a word

or words in a sentence in order to render its meaning clear and intelligible.

Inflection is the rising and falling of the voice which interprets the quality of the thought.

Tone color is expression through the voice of the emotional quality of the thought.

Suppose we use for analysis that familiar line, "Homeward the plowman wends his weary way," and see how the thought expressed in it can be changed by the use of these three qualities. The dropping or downward inflection is the one that gives emphasis. Apply this inflection, giving special emphasis to the word "homeward," and the picture is immediately dominated by the thought that the man is going home. You picture the little cottage, the set table, the cheery fire and the wife and children awaiting his coming. Now do not drop the inflection till you reach the word "weary," and see how the picture changes. All you see now is the long day's tramp over the plowed field. You see the drooping shoulders and the slow, heavy gait of the man weary with the toil of the day. Change the inflection again by giving the word "home" a downward tendency, the rest of the sentence an upward inflection, and you have a question as to whether the man is going home or elsewhere. And so you may experiment with the other compound words in the sentence, always finding that a different inflection or emphasis will call up in the mind an entirely different aspect of the thought. For the tone color, first read it as a mere statement of fact; then read it, feeling in the word "homeward" all the relief and anticipation the man feels as he walks along, and put it into your expression of the word. Feel, as you say the word "weary," the tiredness of the man, the cessation of effort, the relaxation of the mind and body that comes with the knowledge that the day's work is over. And then over all the sentence show the stillness of the evening, the loneliness of the country road, the darkening sky, the far-away barking of a dog, or the occasional bleat of a single sheep. That is tone color, the picture painting quality in the voice. These are the qualities that give individuality and charm to the few voices that portray them.

The best advice I can give you if you wish to develop these vocal powers is to read aloud for a specific time every day, trying as you read, not to impart information, but to call up pictures in the mind of the listener, interpretive reading rather than mere statistical reading, and when you can show these qualities in your reading you will find they will unconsciously become also a part of your everyday conversational interpretation.

In the business world an agreeable, expressive voice and good diction have a distinct commercial value. The salesman whose voice is pleasant to listen to, who has trained his voice unconsciously to respond to every thought and emotion as it comes to him, knows how often the sale is made on these things and not on the customer's desire for the goods. Be cheerful, let your voice reflect your cheerfulness, and it will induce the same spirit in your clients. No one wants to listen to tired, indifferent, discouraged voices one so often has to endure in business. If you do not like your present position, hold in your mind the picture of the things you are aspiring to. Let your voice reflect the hope that is in you, the determination to succeed, the foreshadowing already of the good that is coming. You cannot employ a surer method of bringing it to you.

Respect yourself and others will respect you. Have a definite aim in life, and let your voice show it. I have heard men boast that nothing was too good for them, when apparently all refinement and beauty of speech was so much too good for them that they had never even caught the faintest whisper of its desirability. I have heard a woman repeat "I am a lady born" until I wanted to tell her that if she would learn to speak well one might believe it without having to be informed. Don't be a prig, but be the best you are able to make of yourself.

Remember it is what you are that counts, not what you have. Let your voice reflect dignity, energy, hope, determination, and quiet, collected strength of mind. The very effort so to discipline your voice will help to inculcate these virtues into your character.

A melodious, responsive voice is the one grace

that lasts. Age only softens the voice that has been properly produced and harmoniously used in earlier years. It does not rob it of its beauty and charm of expression.

PART THREE

Self-Expression

NOTE.—The three following chapters are addressed primarily to women. The principles discussed, however, and most of the practical suggestions are of equal value to both men and women.

CHAPTER VII

PERFECT POISE

A Long Mirror and an Open Mind—How You Should Walk and Sit—Facial Expression—Be Convincing.

THE strongest desire and impulse of the human heart is self-expression. It is the unconscious motive behind every act, the unconscious stimulus of every thought. It is as though the human body, the human brain, even the human emotions, were but instruments, machines, through which that mysterious, elusive something, call it soul, or ego, or anything you please, which is the real person, presses and urges its way into a sort of realization of itself in this complex human life.

This is the view I want you to take of the development of personality. Do not think of it as something you can make. Think of it as something you already are and have, but for the perfect expression of which you must provide healthy, harmonious, well-controlled human "instruments." Quite often people who afterward prove to be most charming personalities repulse one at first because they are physically awkward and ungraceful. This is quite unnecessary. Physical grace is only another name for muscular control, and vocal beauty but an understanding and control of the physical organs of speech. Each is within the reach of everyone, varying in degree, perhaps, but still possible.

In the preceding departments of this book we have laid the foundation of both physical and vocal freedom and strength. We have found that the exercise of the muscles has resulted in an unconscious ease and grace of movement, and that the vocal exercises have freed and enlarged the tone and induced natural and correct sound production and flexibility.

Our next step in developing personality is to learn to use this new poise to the best advantage.

In this section I am going to treat our subject from a new standpoint. So far we have considered the value of personality almost entirely from the commercial standpoint. Here we shall study its value as a personal asset, in its relation to our own happiness rather than as a medium for business success.

We gain our first impressions of people from the way they stand, walk and sit, from the chance gesture or the expression of the face. First impressions are important because they have a disconcerting habit of sticking. This means that we must get acquainted with ourselves; find out what sort of first impression we give. There is just one way, and only one, in which we *can* find out. It is useless to ask our friends. They daren't tell us, because so few of us are big enough to bear the truth about ourselves from others. Our only hope for improvement lies in a long mirror and an open mind.

Arrange your mirror, if possible, directly across the room opposite the door. Place a chair within the line of reflection, but not directly between the door and the mirror. Now we are going to use a little imagination, pretend, like the children do, and our little play is going to show us ourselves "as others see us." Imagine you are receiving a friend, someone of whom you are very fond and whom you have not seen for some time. She is standing near the mirror so as you cross to welcome her you are directly reflected in it. So much for the setting. Now open the door, and with both hands extended in cordial welcome, and your face glowing with love and good fellowship, cross the room, greet your friend, invite her to be seated and seat yourself in the chair you have previously placed. Keep your eyes on the mirror and carefully watch four points: your walk, your arm gesture, the expression of your face, and the way you sit.

Before we can properly judge the result of our little trial, we must fix a standard from which to judge. We will begin with the walk. You will remember that in the first article we learned that it was vitally important to carry the weight on the balls of the feet. If this is done, the heel and toe of the extended foot will strike the ground at the same instant, not, as is almost invariably the case with untrained people, heel first. The leg should swing free from the hips, and as the extended foot touches the ground the heel of the other should rise, throwing the weight forward onto the toe preparatory to carrying it forward for the next step. Both heels should never be on the ground at the same time, even for the fraction of a second, and the extended toe should always be pointed downward. If the weight is properly placed, the chest will be carried well forward so that if you should walk up to a wall the chest would strike it first. I remember one of my earlier teachers used to say, "The secret of grace in walking is to keep the chest up and the toes down."

Next in our little self-examination comes the method of sitting. The chief thing here to avoid is the ugly doubling up movement so many people seem to find necessary before being able to sit down. This is quite needless and very ungraceful. The back from the hips to the head should remain easily erect. If you find yourself addicted to an unbecoming habit, practice sitting in this way. Stand in front of your chair and let the back of the right leg lightly touch the frame, keeping the weight well on the ball of the right foot. (You see even here it is important that the weight is correctly placed.) Now place the toe of the left foot under the chair, and as you sit down the weight will be gradually transferred from the right to the left foot. There must not be the slightest bend of the body forward and the left foot must support the weight strongly enough so that you do not " flop " into the chair, but gracefully sink into position. Once experience the real comfort of this perfect poise in walking and sitting and you will never allow yourself to slide back into the old ungraceful ways.

It is a little difficult to dissect faults of gesture, they are so individual. It is perhaps easier to describe what the movement should be than what it should not. Since the gesture is one of welcome, the whole movement of the body should be forward; the arms should be slightly flexed at the elbows, the extended hands turned palms upward, slightly facing each other and about the width of the body apart. If you found your gesture stiff and ungainly, lacking in warmth and feeling, the following exercises will soften your elbows, loosen your wrists, and lend to every movement the charm that comes only of perfect freedom and spontaneity. Place the backs of the hands together, fingers pointed downward, in front of and close to the body, about at the waistline. Now bring the hands straight up in front until they are straight above the head as far as they will go without stiffening the elbows, letting the hands gradually come apart so that at the highest point only the tips of the fingers are touching. Be sure that you do not bend backward from the shoulders as you raise the hands. Instead the chest should come forward slightly. Now draw the arms apart and out at the sides, turn the hands over so that the palms face downward, let the arms sink down to the sides and return to the original position, with the hands back to back in front of the waist-line. This will have made a complete circle, and may be repeated a number of times in succession to give control of arm movement. At no time should the elbows become stiff. See that they are always slightly flexed.

Extend the arms in front of the body with the hands hanging limply from the wrists and about a foot away from each other. Raise the arms, letting the wrists lead, and keeping the chest well forward until they are straight above the head. Now let the hands, still limp, fall back so that the palms face upward, and bring the arms down in front to original position. Do not let the elbows spread apart as you bring the arms down. Keep them well toward each other, otherwise the exercise will be of no value. Be sure also that the chest comes forward and that the hands are limp. You will notice that I am laying much insistence on refraining from bending backward when the arms are being raised. I have found this tendency to bend back distressingly common, and certainly the effects are sufficiently injurious as to warrant some special attention. As the unfortunate result of centuries of wearing artificial support in the shape of corsets, etc., the modern woman's back is unnaturally weak and sensitive. Nature is an economist of the first order, and will not go on indefinitely providing muscular strength which is not utilized. It is just such habits as the one we are discussing which force an unnatural strain on one set of muscles to the exclusion of the muscles that properly should be employed, that is responsible for much of the nervous debility so prevalent among women. Figures 11 and 12 accompanying Chapter III show the correct and incorrect methods of raising the arms. Try it for yourself the next time you put on your hat or do your hair. Notice the strain on the abdominal muscles and in the small of the back when you adopt the old incorrect posture. Then try the correct way, with the chest well forward, and the back and head erect. You immediately feel a sense of poise and strength and repose, entirely free from any sort of strain, that convinces you more thoroughly than any argument could do, of the injury you have unconsciously been doing yourself.

We have yet one more point of self-criticism, and that by no means the least important, facial expression. What was your verdict in this respect? Did you discover yourself to be one of the innumerable multitude who go through life with faces like death masks, unintelligent, unfeeling, unresponsive? If so, there is just one hope for you, one way in which you can redeem yourself from the worse than uninteresting mass of people whose eyes and faces seem the shutters rather than the windows of the soul. Make out a list of emotions you want to portray—anger, fear, love, hatred, bewilderment, surprise, disdain, and so on. If it will help your imagination, make a little story involving such feelings and then arrange them on your list in the sequence followed in your little tale. Then stand before your mirror and try to let your face tell the story. Think how much the moving picture actor has to portray by facial expression and don't get discouraged because you find that at first anger, hatred and disdain seem all one to you, and that love and pity seem hopelessly inseparable. Just persist, and in a little time you will find that the thought of any emotion calls up a corresponding expression in your eyes and gradually your face will become the sensitive, living reflection of your mind, lending your conversation a vitality and charm that is the very essence of personality. Just one word of warning, however. Do not try to cultivate a set expression to suggest any particular emotion. Nothing is more irritating than a face that is constantly grimacing. Try to feel the emotion and then wait for it to flow into the face. Each time, as you feel the face warming and changing to the expression of emotion, try to pour more and more feeling into it, so that at last each thought as it comes immediately surcharges the whole countenance with radiant responsiveness, giving it a beauty and magnetism infinitely to be preferred to the doll-like prettiness of perfect, if empty, features.

CHAPTER VIII

BE NATURAL

Overcome the Barriers that Confine Your Personality—The Value of Controlled Emotion—Freedom and Laughter.

AN old conundrum worthy of resurrection runs, "What is the keynote of good manners?" and the answer is "B natural." To be natural is the one essential quality you must insist upon if you would be magnetic. To be natural means to be sincere, and sincerity, like charity, "covereth a multitude of sins." That is why personality must be developed from within. Time spent in cultivating little airs and graces, facial tricks, magazine cover poses, and so on is worse than wasted. Nothing is so readily recognized as spurious as an imitated or cultivated mannerism. This applies to the voice as well as to the body. I have heard women at clubs and social affairs who were absolutely uninteresting and even boring, notwithstanding most exquisitely trained and modulated voices, because one was conscious all the time that they were not trying to convey some absorbing idea, but only trying to show what beautiful sounds they could make. On the stage we call this "listening to the sound of one's voice," and many a promising young actress has failed to realize her brightest hopes because she did not remember that art is not art until it becomes unconscious; that the well-trained body and the cultured voice are just instruments, perfected mediums through which the great burning passions of humanity must be able to pour themselves freely and unconsciously. It is true that through long experience the accomplished actress will learn how, both physically and vocally, to portray an emotion she may at the moment be feeling very little, but the element of sincerity will be there, because she employs the action or tone she knows she herself would use were she that person under those circumstances. That is why she can carry conviction to her audience.

But the commonest and most fatal form of unnaturalness is not affectation, but what we might call subnaturalness. Many people lack all force of magnetism because they are so shut in and surrounded by a wall of self-consciousness and self-distrust that their friends rarely, and their general acquaintances never, penetrate to the real personality. But the life behind the apparently colorless, unresponsive exterior is often very eager, the intellect keen, and the emotions really vivid, in spite of this barrier of reserve. It is these people to whom the work advocated in these chapters will come as an angel of deliverance, setting free the imprisoned mind, and letting it out into the full sunshine of life.

Delsarte's motto was: "Be strong at the center and you will be free at the circumference." Physical exercise strengthens and equalizes the body so that the movement of the hands and head become unconscious and graceful. Vocal exercises make of the voice an equally responsive instrument. But after we have perfected the instruments, there must still be something else. There must be feeling and thought, the motive power of all speech and action. You see we really are working backward from effect to cause instead of from cause to effect. But in taking up the physical and vocal work first we were simply opening the safety valve before increasing the steam pressure.

The expression of emotion is taught in all schools of dramatic education by means of pantomime and monologue. Pantomime is most useful because the endeavor to express a story or emotion without the assistance of the voice intensifies the physical and facial characteristics. Let me give you a sample story, one that you can work out for yourself.

The pantomimists are not allowed to use "properties"; the imagination is stimulated much more if they are not used, but if you find it easier at first to use a real table, vases, letter and flowers, it is quite permissible to do so. Also no words are used, only sounds to express emotion, such as cries, shrieks, moans or laughter.

Now for the story: A woman, young, happy, humming a little lilting love song, her arms full of flowers just picked from the garden, enters the room with the assured ease and confidence which bespeak the mistress of the house. She walks to the center-table, and before laying her burden down she revels for a moment in long-drawn inhalations of their fragrance. Then, still with happy, smiling lips humming a little love song, she goes to the mantelshelf and takes from the right end and the middle a pair of vases, which she carries to the table and fills with blossoms. She carries them back to the mantel, places them in their original position, and extends her hand to take the one in the left corner, when the movement is arrested by the sight of a letter standing behind the vase. The little song dies, the smile fades from her lips, as she takes the letter in her hand, and at first curiously, and then with dawning suspicion, examines the writing. It is addressed to her husband, but some instinct tells her that the innocent-looking missive contains a menace to her happiness. She turns it over, examines it from all angles, holds it up to the light trying to see the size of the contents, dallying with the temptation to open it. At last she almost decides not to yield, but changes her mind in the very act of returning the letter to the mantel, and after a guilty glance round the room to see that she is not watched, she hurriedly tears it open and reads it. Her instinct is correct, and as she reads, her face slowly settles into an expression of frozen horror. She drops the letter and walks toward the door in a wavering, uncertain way like a somnambulist, but before she reaches it, as the full realization of some awful tragedy opens out to her heart and brain, with a gasping cry she sinks unconscious to the floor.

In this little story, which takes but a few moments to enact, lie unlimited possibilities of expression. All the changes should be very gradual, but very intense. More important than anything else, *feel.* Let the story live to you, so that every emotion is not hers, but your own. Our emotions die, as everything in nature dies, if they are not used, and no one in whom the emotions are half petrified can possibly possess the vivid fire of life that for want of a better name we call magnetism. Act this little tale over and over until you express in face and movement each succeeding feeling so truthfully that were a picture taken and thrown on the screen no words would be needed to interpret its meaning. Remember it is freedom we are trying to gain—freedom from restricting habits, freedom to let the thoughts and emotions of our inner selves out into the light of life. And as you work out these little stories you will find that the abandonment you gain begins to reflect in your everyday character. Every idea comes to you accompanied by a corresponding glow of feeling that makes the most trivial action instinct with meaning. And with the increase in the ability to feel comes an increase in the ability to express the feeling. One becomes so accustomed to expression in working out the little stories that every feeling soon awakens an eager responsiveness that destroys forever every symptom of self-consciousness.

Don't make all your stories tragedies. Laughter is the great medicine of life, mental as well as physical. The cheerful, happy, smiling woman is a perennial tonic to everyone about her. Novelists and poets may paint pretty pictures for us of victories won over the sterner sex through April tears and pouting lips, but every woman of experience knows that these are very frail weapons, useful only while love is very young, and that the ready, sympathetic, understanding smile is infinitely more lasting and irresistible. Full, free, spontaneous laughter is almost a lost art in these days of restraint and pressure. One of the first selections I give a pupil is always a monologue or story that requires unrestrained laughter. Invariably the same look of appealing consternation comes to every pair of eyes, the same distressed cry from every pair of lips, "I am sorry, but I can't laugh. I just can't." Of course they can't, but they learn, and they learn in this way: Using the octave "C" as a guide, sing "Ha" first down the scale several times, then up the scale several times, giving a distinct little pressure from the diaphragm to every note. When you can execute this freely as an exercise, leave the music, and increase the time until it develops into laughter, when you will, of course, not try to retain any suggestion of the exercise, neither time, number of notes, nor scale. The exercise should free the diaphragm and the throat, not serve as a foundation on which to build the sort of false, affected imitation laugh that is so irritating when we get it from across the footlights.

Again I must say to you, see that your ideals are as high as you are capable of imagining them. We seldom reach our ideals. As we grow toward them they rise higher and higher, so that the attainment that would have thrilled us with pride and gratification at a lower stage of development, means to us when it comes merely a stepping stone to the greater thing we have grown in the meantime to desire. The higher your aim, the higher will your attainment be. Satisfaction with oneself means the cessation of growth.

Cultivate the society of people who reflect the qualities you desire to possess. Imitation is unconscious sometimes, but it is always one of the strongest forces that affect us. The man who prefers to be a big fish in a little puddle has reached the fullest capacity of his growth. We learn by the association of those who know more than we do, not by patronizing those who know less.

CHAPTER IX

EMOTION

The Receptive Mood—Physical and Emotional Response to Music; to Rhythm—The Interpretation of Emotion.

HAVE we forgotten how to feel? Life today is so external that it almost seems as though we had. But our magnetic ideal will not be realized unless every part of our nature is developed, the emotional as well as the physical and mental.

We must know how to feel, to feel keenly, but also to control our feelings. Are you looking at a beautiful painting? Don't merely catalogue it in your mind. Sit down before it and let it sink into your soul. See the sunset as a real thing, not as exquisite painted coloring. Go up on the hill-top with the artist. Sit with him there until the vision he saw of the opening of the heavens thrills your own feeling into responsiveness.

There are some feelings that we can neither put into word nor into action, and they are sometimes the very deepest, most sacred feelings of which the soul is capable. There are the unconscious depths from which our more familiar and external characteristics spring.

Did you ever stand alone on the seashore and let

the song of the mighty ocean fill your soul with its transcendent melody? You look out to the horizon across the roaring, foaming billows, and you know that far, far beyond your vision still rolls and tosses this great mass of living water. And your soul is thrilled with a sense of the insignificance of the trivialities of life, and some glimpse of the destiny of man, the reflection of the Creator of all this power and might and wonder comes to you, so that you go home conscious of a strange uplift that helps you to see above and beyond the petty annoyance of the daily grind, that helps to keep you in that perfect poise which is the essence of individuality.

It is in moments like these, when all that is external is forgotten, when the inner self is bathed in the glory of its natural life, that we gain the perspective that is needed if we are to make of ourselves all we are capable of becoming.

We are told that light, heat, color, sound are but different rates of vibration. Health in the individual means a normal rate of vibration. Certain diseases can be cured by the use of power-rays of light, the light vibrations serving to raise the vibrations of the depleted or unhealthy body. In the same way experiments are being made abroad with music as the curative element. The basic idea is the same, the value of vibration, but music and color have an emotional and mental effect as well as a physical one. Under the influence of music the physical, emotional and mental are harmoniously and equably stimulated, for the moment bringing the triple nature up to its highest possible rate of vibration.

This is the object of all self-culture. Every individual has a special, personal rate of vibration. When thought, feeling and action are well trained, free and spontaneous, a condition results of perfect equilibrium and poise which is a very fountain of energy, a radiant, vital force as real and vivid as a current of electricity. It expresses itself physically in the nobility of the uplifted chest, an elation of movement that seems to spurn the earth beneath the foot. It shows in the quick sympathy of feeling, the ready response to the joy, the sorrow, the love of others. It betrays itself in the quick, keen grasp of ideas by the mind, the clear, unbiased judgment, the understanding comprehension of one's fellowman. And behind and through it all you sense the clean, strong soul, holding all these, its servants, in calm, assured, unafraid control.

The word "harmony" suggests to one's mind a sister word, the word "rhythm." The sense of rhythm is universal. It is a law of nature. The recurring seasons wax and wane in unchanging, unbroken rhythm. Night and day mark the pulse-beats of nature. The soft lapping of the silver sea whispering through the semi-darkness of a summer night; the budding, the flowering, the falling leaf; the unfathomable mystery of birth and death—all these come to us as pulsations of the great heart of the universe.

Our bodies are governed by rhythmic law. The heart beats, the lungs inflate and depress, the body demands nourishment through sensation of hunger and thirst, demands sleep to rebuild the wasted energies, with well-defined and systematic periodicity.

The one perfect medium for the expression of the inborn sense of rhythm that exists impartially in every race of the human family lies in the dance. The character of a nation is portrayed in its dances. As a nation we have not yet established a definite and individual dance, if we exclude, as we are glad to do, the temporary indulgence in the objectionable rag-time sex dances which travelers abroad are ashamed to hear described as "American." The real tendency with us seems to be in the direction of interpretive dancing, and of all types none can be more beautiful, useful or truthful than interpretive, dramatic dancing. It is the logical sequence and development of education for self-expression. It is perhaps the only form of expression that gives scope for full mental, emotional and physical freedom at the same moment. I recently attended a most interesting exhibition of a system of eurhythmics, which begins as a form of physical training or movement to music, and develops into something that is scarcely an interpretive dance and yet is something more than pantomime to music. In many ways it was more pleasing than a dance because of the absolute control and co-ordination of muscular action. Much could be done along these lines by the independent student, especially one who has followed the preparatory work given in these articles. Select your music, and let the effect on your emotional nature suggest some story or situation to you. When this is established, sink yourself into the character and let the rhythm and development of the theme control your movements. Don't try for stage effects, don't try to think too much; just obey the suggestion of the music, even though at first the movement may be very slight. As you accustom yourself to the sensation of abandonment, the impulse to movement will increase and clarify, and the story will open out to you from every aspect, offering an avenue for the expression of every thought and emotion.

One of the finest selections at the exhibition I have mentioned was the characterization of a manacled prisoner. To the accompaniment of slow, soft music the curtain rises to disclose a man, his hands bound behind his back, lying outstretched on the floor. For a moment he lies there quietly, apparently asleep, but presently, as the music strengthens, he begins to stir, painfully and laboriously. Slowly, with every evidence of great weakness, he staggers first to his knees and at last to his feet, where he stands for a moment struggling to maintain his balance. Then, with lagging steps, bent back and hanging head, he begins to pace back and forth across his cell, at each turn lifting his head and body in an abandonment of despair. Soon his mood changes, and he pauses in the middle of the room and begins to struggle to burst his bonds. To and fro his body sways as he bends every effort toward regaining his freedom. He kneels on the floor, endeavoring to conserve his strength, and at last with one great effort the ropes that bind him give way, his hands are free. For a second he kneels there almost stupefied, unable to believe his good fortune; then, as the knowledge reaches his mind, there comes with it a fictitious strength that brings him leaping to his feet, his freed hands raised high in the air, his whole attitude expressing the fierce joy of a wild animal. But slowly the realization comes to him that freeing his hands after all avails him very little, so long as he is confined in his cell, and now he gives way to a very madness of rage and despair, directing his fury toward the little door that shuts him away from the life of his kind. But, as he feels the hopelessness of his situation, his rage dies, the spasmodic energy fades, leaving him weaker and more broken than before. Slowly he sinks again to his knees, every line of face and body expressing a very agony of helpless despair; gradually the tension slackens, his whole frame loosens, he sinks forward on his elbow, and then once more he stretches himself out upon the floor, the last twitching muscle relaxes, and the end is the same as the beginning, except that now he sleeps his last sleep and has won his eternal freedom.

This is an example of interpretive pantomime

to music. One must guard against losing the strength of the dramatic element through too close attention to the rhythm of the sound, but if the rhythm is established first, and then the full abandonment given to the emotional quality, the dramatic force need not be affected. Many very beautiful little situations can be worked out in this way, and one's favorite musical selections made to live in a much more personal and intense way. A very charming and delicate little pantomime was that employed by Sir Herbert Tree in his production in London of "The Darling of the Gods." A little Japanese maiden is at play in her father's garden when she spies a butterfly flitting from flower to flower. She leaves her play and begins to follow it, running after it as it flies to another blossom, creeping up to try to surprise it after it has settled, snatching at it with her little brown hand. At last she manages to capture the pretty creature, and she kneels down on the ground in Japanese fashion and opens her hand slowly to examine her prisoner. But as the beautiful painted wings make no movement toward escape, the happy smile changes to a look of consternation and fear, and when she opens her hand fully and discovers that her pretty plaything is dead and that no petting or pleading can again send the life palpitating through the little body, her grief and self-reproach find relief in a passionate burst of tears.

The value of working out of these little stories

lies in the element of freedom they give, not only to the physical, but to the emotional also. The essence of individuality or personality rests in the soul, in the "I am" of every man that marks him out as different to his fellows, in the intelligence that guides and utilizes the thought, feeling and action of the body. Nevertheless, that soul can only grow and expand by means of the experiences it gains in this world, and it can only attain its fullest growth when its vehicles are fully under its control. To cultivate the mind by reading, study and discussion; to free and enlarge the emotions by broadening and deepening our sympathies, and encouraging a keen and ready response to the joys and sorrows of others; to make of the body a clean, strong, healthy, sensitive instrument, means to make of the triune nature a channel through which the strong soul may pour itself out freely, gladly, spontaneously, keying the whole personality into such tensity and vibrancy that the power of its magnetism radiates out as a vital force affecting everyone with whom it comes in contact. This is the secret of real beauty and charm, freedom of expression.

PART FOUR

Mental Power

CHAPTER X

THE ATTITUDE TOWARD YOUR WORK

A Man Becomes Like the Company He Keeps—Inspiring Others in Your Office—Concentration: Its Importance and How to Acquire It—Do You Waste Time?

IN the City of New York, the president of one of its most important and powerful banks has his office arranged in an unusual and effective way. His desk is placed on a shallow platform, not high enough to make it necessary to invite his visitor to share it, but just high enough to make the man who is sitting on the floor level feel a suggestion of inferiority. With the light so arranged that his own features are in the shadow and his visitor's face fully exposed, this man, whose name is known the world over in financial circles, sits behind his elevated desk, and like the Egyptian Sphinx betrays nothing of his own sentiments or ideas, while he draws from his visitor all he can be induced to tell.

This is a practical demonstration of the value of a knowledge of the psychology of the human mind. The physical necessity of looking up to the man behind the desk suggests a corresponding mental condition. It suggests the idea of being before a judge, and increases the fear of adverse decision. To make a proposition positive and attractive under these conditions means that it must have a good, sound foundation, and even then may suffer from the self-consciousness induced in its advocate by the unusual condition of environment.

There is the same kind of value in the possession of well-developed, assured physical poise. Keep your chest up, your back straight, your head erect, and you will inspire confidence and respect. Respect yourself, and others will respect you. That does not mean either that you should be a prig. Self-respect is not conceit. The man who is always advertising to the world how much he knows is the man who knows very little. The man who really knows, knows also that the amount he has learned of the world's store of knowledge is but an infinitesimal part of the whole. It is only the teachable mind that learns. The cock-sure man, who prides himself on never changing his opinion, has reached the limit of his development.

Keep an unbiased mind. Let life be your teacher. Learn sometimes by the other fellow's mistakes. Don't always have to put your own hand into the fire to be convinced that it burns. Learn, too, from the other fellow's success. Don't be ashamed to sit at the feet of the mighty. A man is not only known by the company he keeps, but he becomes like the company he keeps. The least member of a company of intellectual giants is going to learn a great deal more than the biggest man in a company of ineffectives. Don't look at yourself as a part of a big, struggling mass, out of which so few men are doomed to climb that it may well happen your name may not be among them. Think of your present condition as a mere temporary one. Don't count it your eternal home. Think of yourself as already the thing you want to become; of your work as a stepping stone to the higher thing.

There is all the difference in the world between the man who goes to the office in the morning with the feeling that there's another day to drag through, another lot of work to be plowed over, and the man who feels that this is his opportunity to prove his value, to make a step up to the higher place he has in sight. The first man's eyes are dull, his step lagging, his whole deportment a weary protest against the monotony of life. The second man doesn't know that life is monotonous. He never has time to find it out. To him each new day is an opportunity for achievement, perhaps the guardian of the moment that shall mark another milestone in his career.

When this man enters his office in the morning, even the office boy feels it. Coming in with a full, swinging stride, his whole body alert and poised, his eyes shining with interest and ambition, he radiates a magnetic energy and determination that become a fountain of inspiration to all who are associated with him. His superiors have confidence in him, because they respect the fact that he is going to get on for his own sake, and he cannot make the best of himself without also doing the best thing for them. He is the man they will advance when the position ahead of him is vacant. He is the man they will absorb into the firm rather than have him go out as a competitor. He will be too valuable from the first position he holds with them to have them willing to lose him and his ability to a competitor.

This man will never tell you he lost his position because the head of the department was jealous of him. He knows that employers want efficiency, and that they keep and promote the man who gives them what they want. He knows, too, that business efficiency is the outcome of mental efficiency. His mind is his own, and he takes care that it is efficient. His brain is the flaming sword with which he may force his path to the faraway heights. He sees to it that this invaluable instrument is made more effective by reading the right sort of books, by contact, through conversation, with men of keen intellect and judicial mind. He learns to concentrate. He does not allow his mind to wander hither and thither at its own will. He is its master. It thinks as he directs it. He masters his destiny because he has mastered himself.

When the children of Great Britain are being taught the history of their country, they are told a little story they love of one of their early English heroes, the story of King Alfred in the goat-herd's cottage. Being unaware of the royal station of the fugitive, the wife of the goat-herd asked the King to watch the cakes she had placed on the stone to cook, while she went to draw water. When she returned, the cakes were burned, and she rewarded her visitor's negligence with a sound box on the ears. The King had been so absorbed in his plans for the routing of his enemies, who had recently defeated him in battle, that he had forgotten the cakes. But out of his absorption grew the idea that he shortly afterward put into effect and whose success cleared his country of his foes. The cakes were sacrificed but the idea survived.

This is efficiency. So to concentrate on the thing you are doing that for the time being nothing else exists. It is not easy to cultivate this ability to focus the mind exclusively on one point. It means the constant and determined elimination of the cakes of life until the proper time for their consideration arrives. It means winning the hardest fight a man has to make, the fight with himself.

Concentration is the first essential of mental power, to be able to hold one's mind against the distraction of outer stimulus. If you would learn how difficult this is, and also how valuable a quality it is to possess, test it in this way. You may eliminate the possibility of outer distraction as much as you can by shutting yourself into a room alone. You may choose a comfortable chair, and relax your body. You may even shut your eyes, so that nothing you might see may distract you. Now think of some abstract quality—love, justice, truthfulness, charity, any of these ideas—and fix your thought upon it to the exclusion of everything else. Try to see its value as a personal asset, its effect on humanity, the result of its use in business and social life. Try to feel it until it seems to become a composite part of your own nature.

You won't get very far the first time. For a few minutes you will seem to be doing quite nicely, and then suddenly you will awake to find yourself thinking of something that happened today or yesterday at the office or elsewhere or something you expect to happen tomorrow. You will seize your refractory mind and bring it sharply back to its original point, only to discover in a few minutes that the same thing has happened and you are idly thinking of other things again.

Do not give up because you found it difficult. A race-horse is not made the first time he is ridden. You may consider if you allowed yourself to think of a concrete thing, instead of what may seem an uninteresting idea, you would get better results. But it is with the hard thing to do that the overcoming gives strength. It is easy to think the thing that interests us for the moment. But if you would have your mind an efficient instrument, ready to obey your orders at any time to the best advantage, you must make it do the things it does not want to do.

You must master it. You must not allow it to master you.

Conceding the fact, as we must in the face of all the proofs of modern thought and experience, that our destiny is mind-created and mind-limited, then it is time more specific attention should be paid to the conservation of this inestimable quality. In and about our large cities, New York, Chicago, Philadelphia and others, thousands and thousands of people spend daily from half an hour to two hours on the cars and trains going to and returning from their places of employment. The man who lives an hour's ride from his work spends twelve hours a week, or six hundred and twenty-four hours a year on the cars. Counting a working day of eight hours, this man spends seventy-eight full working days, or two months and eighteen working days riding backward and forward. Almost a quarter of a year of working time, and what use does he make of it?

Here is your chance for developing thought power. First try to shut out the distractions of the people and things around you. Instead of idly looking out of the window and allowing thought currents to vaguely drift through your mind, determine to think of one special thing. When you find your mind wandering, as it will at first, bring it sternly back to the subject under consideration. If something happens that seems worth thinking about, drop the other train of thought and devote your mental attention to the new thing. The chief thing to watch is that the thing you are thinking about, whatever it may happen to be, gets your undivided attention. With two months and eighteen days of full working time at your disposal, in a year the increased power and control of your mind will mean an increase in your salary check.

There is but one royal road to success; that road is self-culture. Self-culture is mind-culture. When you have trained your mind, and hold it in obedience, you have in your possession the unfailing and unconquerable weapon that will vanquish failure and set you securely on the high throne of your desire.

CHAPTER XI

SELF-CONFIDENCE

Think for Yourself—How to Overcome Fear—Convince Yourself—Build Success Thoughts.

ONE of the most impressive sights to be found the world over is the Statue of Liberty, in New York harbor. Her large, calm, gracious dignity of bearing is the result of perfect physical poise, and equalized strength. In her uplifted hand she holds the signal of her office, the light which only liberty can throw into the dark places of the world. In the nobility of her bearing one sees the reflection of the knowledge of the artist of the greatness of the idea he must convey—not only political and economic freedom, but that which is greater than all—freedom of mind and thought.

Let the Statue of Liberty inspire you as she inspires the immigrant. To him she means the leaving behind of all the old methods of government, of all the old traditions. He has been bound by unjust laws, by hard class conditions. She tells him that a man is an individual, not a mere part of a mass. She promises him all of success that he can make for himself. She gives him the freedom of opportunity.

You also have been bound. You have been bound and limited by the thoughts that others have formulated for you. Thoughts of old age, of sickness, of failure. Leave these old thoughts behind. They are not for you. For you the glorious light of a new liberty is shining—the liberty to fix your own condition through the exercise of your own mind. Let go of all your old conditions. You are your own taskmaster, your own slave-driver. Cease thinking thoughts of hardship and fear. Know that no failure can touch you, that nothing can touch you that can harm you.

Let us assume that there is a constantly recurring situation to which you always look forward with dread. It may be there is some man with whom you have to do business of whom you have always had a certain fear. It may be your employer, or your largest customer. You don't know just why, but you have always failed to be convincing when talking to him.

Don't keep struggling to overcome this fear, this embarrassment, in the same old way. Reason it out. You know you are right, that your arguments are as good as his. Then why isn't he convinced? Because he senses that in the back of your mind you are doubtful of your ability to convince him.

You will never conquer this situation until you have fought the thing out with yourself. On the morning of your next appointment with him, arise with the firm determination to make the meeting successful today. Today will be a fresh start. Say to yourself that you are meeting him today for the first time. Remember, the control of the situation is mental. Then you must prepare for it from this standpoint. While you are getting ready for the interview, repeat this thought until it becomes an incorporate part of your mind attitude: "I shall succeed, I am all that this man is, I am power." Such thoughts as these, firmly held, will invest you with a quiet dignity and conscious strength, that will shock your man out of his former estimate of you into a conviction that you mean what you say.

Self-confidence means the difference between a restricted and a developed personality. Keep constantly convincing yourself that you have no fear, that you are bound to succeed, that you won't acknowledge obstacles.

Avoid, as you would the pestilence, two things—fear and anger. Scientific investigation has proven that these two excesses engender poisons in the body that destroy its health, and break down its efficiency. If thought can cure, thought can also destroy. Strong thoughts of fear have been known to kill people, as also have intense fits of anger. You would not willingly take small doses of poison. Don't indulge in small doses of these poisons either. If you are right, you do not need to be angry. If you are wrong, you cannot afford to be.

The effect of fear is psychological as well as physiological. When you fear a thing, you are making a mental picture of that thing or condition that will prove to be the easiest way of bringing that thing or condition to you. Nature's laws are all two-edged. You can use them to fight for you, or you may turn them on yourself and rend yourself with them. Affirmative thoughts of good make you positive, make of you a magnetic center to which good things are attracted. Thoughts of fear and worry make you negative, a prey for every ill that burdens the mental atmosphere around you.

Recognize your fundamental equality with the greatest man that lives. He has nothing to draw on that you may not have if you take yourself in hand and develop your powers. Do not think you are limited by heredity, by environment. The thoughts of your forefathers can only limit you as you consent to go on generating those thoughts. Think your own thoughts, and refuse to be limited by thoughts that others have set in motion for you.

Examine yourself for the causes of your lack of success, and then plan your methods of attacking them. You will not win the fight by guerilla warfare. Only through a well thought out, definite system of campaign, and persistent, sustained action will your battle end in victory. Your chief weapon is the conviction of yourself.

As you do your daily exercise, watch your physical development with the joy of perfect confidence that the condition which you are trying to bring about is steadily arriving. You must remember that the subconscious mind, when untrained, works automatically. If you have been feeding it thoughts of physical sickness and inefficiency for years, it is not going to be turned round and set working in the other direction in a moment. You must think strongly and think persistently. You must talk and think health, strength, poise, constantly and confidently, even in face of the apparent conditions which wrong thinking have forced upon your unfortunate body. Take comfort in the fact that the same force which keeps up an ill condition when you think ill thoughts, will just as automatically and persistently keep up a right condition if you think right thoughts. Your present task is to turn it in the right direction.

Enjoy your work. There is beauty and joy in everything if you will look for it. Work that is loved is half done, before it is begun, and everything in connection with it, well done. Work that is disliked is only half done when it is supposed to be finished. Get something out of everything, even the thing you thought would be unpleasant. It will destroy your distaste for it if you look for the valuable idea behind it.

Begin the day well. During your exercise and bath, affirm the improving condition of your body. Hold your mind in the thought of the health and grace and control you are gaining. Say it over to yourself, again and again, until the idea is unequivocally established. "I am health. I am strength. I am perfect poise." Essentially you are all these things. Your distortions are the result of your own wrong thinking.

Continue your affirmation when you take up your business thoughts. "I am success. I am power. I am the master of my destiny. Victory is mine." Know in your very soul that you will succeed and nothing will be able to stop you. The same great philosopher we have quoted before said that with a grain of faith a man could move a mountain, but nobody believes it. No one ever had a greater knowledge of the laws of nature and the laws of life than He had, and the laws exist the same today as He knew them then.

Without faith in oneself there can be no progress. You must know your own possibilities before you can work to develop them. Know yourself as an unconquerable child of eternity, a being whose only reason for being on this earth at all is that he may learn to use and control the forces that surround him, and your triple nature will respond to your demand, and materialize for you the condition of your inner knowledge. Remember that your mental attitude is going to suggest a corresponding one to the people with whom you associate. Very few people think their own thoughts exclusively. The great mass of people scarcely do any original thinking at all. Even the strongest are affected to some extent by the telepathic influence of others' thoughts.

It is this condition that accounts for national ideals, for mass thought. Constant reading and conversation along any one line will so prejudice a mass of people that they are incapable of thinking justly and with an unbiased attitude of mind on that particular thing. Use this law to your own advantage. By your own thought, by your manner, by your own confidence in your ultimate success, suggest thoughts of success to the people you contact. Their certainty that you are succeeding will react on you and your conditions and help to bring about the very success that they see for you. Nothing succeeds like success, because once set the idea going in the minds of a sufficient number of people, and the thing soon carries itself of its own impetus.

If you are not all you would like yourself to be, build your ideal and then strike boldly out to materialize it. Have the courage of your convictions. You owe it to yourself to leave nothing undone that will tell for your ultimate success. Don't think because you are a business man that grace and poise are all right for people who don't have to work, but that you don't need them. You do need them. It takes a perfection of parts to make a perfect whole. Your physical being should reflect your mental being, not disguise it. Your voice should respond to your mental inspiration, not serve as a muffler to it. Personal development must always proceed along the triple lines of physical, sensational and mental. To cultivate one to the neglect of the others is to limit the one you are cultivating.

CHAPTER XII

DESIRES AND AMBITIONS

Action Impelled by Desire—How Great Is Your Desire?—Have a Mental Picture of What You Intend to Be—Know No Limitations.

SEVERAL years ago, while travelling through Canada, I received an invitation to attend a reception at which a very noted author was to speak. I accepted the invitation with great pleasure, since I had read all the author's works, and was glad of the opportunity to meet him. I admired his books chiefly for their virility, their suggestion of the rugged, open-air life of mountain and lake and forest. I expected to find the author a man of vivid, impelling magnetism, reflecting in himself the virility of those products of his imagination. To my astonishment, I found a man devoid of magnetism, who read his paper from beginning to end without raising his eyes to his audience, possessing a monotonous, colorless voice and a face that was an impassive mask. He was everything his books were not, yet his real self it was that had created his books. What we saw was not the man, but the sheath, the covering that hid the man from us, through which he had been unable to break, the body that should have given him the very instruments he needed to show himself to our minds. If he had not written what was in his soul, we should have judged him to be just what his exterior personality represented him to be.

We cannot all use this medium of expression. There must be some that read as well as some that write books, but that does not mean that we need be content when our real selves remain masked from the outer world. It is only a question of whether your body, your voice, your manners, are going to master you or whether you will master them. Whether they shall be your jailers or your servants.

The force that impels all action is desire. Desire to have, to be, to know, to feel. The higher the form of life, the more varied and complex are its desires. It is not only an impelling force, it is also an attractive element.

One is no longer considered semi-insane when one suggests that thought is creative. The certain success of many branches of mental healing has engendered at least a theoretical and speculative belief that the mind is supreme, or rather can be taught to become so. But it does not require a physical healing to convince any thinker that the real controller of a man's condition and destiny is his thought. It is a most singular thing to me that we have for generations been listening to the most practical and common-sense suggestions along these lines, but have entirely missed their point because we heard them in church, read from the Bible. It has taken the heretic, who could read the Bible for what he found in it, just as he would any other book, to show us some of its truths. Why should we limit such a saying as "As a man thinketh, so is he," to some connection with sowing wild oats. It is true. A man is what he thinks, and the amount of himself he demonstrates in every-day life depends on how hard he thinks it.

Desire is, of course, a mental condition. You may desire food, be hungry, but it is not your body that is desiring. It is your mind that, having received notice from your body that the supply of nourishment is running short, desires to replenish it, and demands food. It is then the impelling force which makes the body seek the food it requires, and suggests methods of obtaining it.

Ambition is desire, the desire for self-expression along the line of least resistance. Desire is a thing to be cultivated. Feed it with the imagination. Do not desire to have. Greed and envy, and a host of allied uglinesses, owe their birth to the desire to have. Desire to be, and the things will come of themselves. To be a great success, a master in your particular business or profession, that is a legitimate desire, an ambition that will be an incentive to the exercise of your highest faculties. To desire to be rich in order that you may possess things, such a desire stunts the mind and tells against success.

The first and most important thing to do with

regard to one's career is to focus one's ambitions. To scatter your energy over a number of things means that none of them is going to get your best work. Be one-pointed. Have a definite mental picture always of the thing you want to become, and that will concentrate your effort toward its realization. You may decide later that this is not the thing you really need after all, and change your course entirely. But the concentration you have exercised in the original desire will stand you in good stead in the new one, and since nothing is lost, and our minds do not after all work in jumps, you will find that the first thing logically led up to the last. It simply meant you had outgrown the first.

When Charles Rann Kennedy, in his great play, "The Servant in the House," makes one of his characters say, "Everything comes true, if you just wish hard enough," he isn't just telling fairy stories. He is teaching a real truth. The trouble with most of us is that we don't wish hard enough to go out and make our wishes come true. It is the supreme wish that impels to action, and that is not always the wish we think we have. You are a salesman, and you think you want to succeed. You know you would rather have more money. You even have quite definite plans as to how you would spend more money if you had it. When other men are talking of their plans and ambitions, you can contribute your share. You really think you are ambitious. But—yesterday it rained. What did you do? You probably had quite a legitimate excuse for staying at home. One day isn't such a big slice out of thirty, and you thought you would make it up by working harder on another and more pleasant day. One can always find excuses, but the real fault is with the desire. You desired comfort and self-indulgence more than you desired business. You will always obey the stronger desire. If you desire success with all your heart and soul and mind and body, not war, nor weather, nor anything in all the world will keep it from you.

Keep your ambitions a long way ahead of you. It will give you perspective. The little things of today will seem smaller when they are but the stepping stones to the greater things of tomorrow. "Hitch your wagon to a star" for the psychological effect it will have on your mind. The higher your aim, the sooner will you spurn the lower reaches. If you have two flights of stairs to climb, you are tired on the first flight, and exhausted by the time you reach the top of the second. If the elevator isn't running, and you have to climb six, the first two are nothing at all, and you don't begin to feel tired until the fourth. Eventually you make the sixth.

The man who understands and uses intelligently this desire-force doesn't waste his time. He knows what he wants, and starts out to get it. When things seem not to be coming to him, he wastes no time in worrying, or in blaming someone else. He knows that the thing he desires is waiting for him. He simply hasn't found the best way to get it.

Desire is will, the wish or will to become something. It is the greatest power in the world. Backed by an understanding of life and its laws, it is unconquerable. There is plenty of everything for everybody. You need not tread on the dead bodies of your fellows to achieve success. You will leave them behind you, but only because they have not developed the power to climb. You are not to blame for their failure. No one else is to blame for yours.

Accept your personal responsibility. Don't talk so much about capital oppressing labor. Most of our capitalists were poor once. The capitalists didn't keep them down. Know yourself an individual power. What others have done, you can do. Arouse your imagination. Picture yourself in your mind the thing you desire to be. Then bend every effort to the materialization of your dream. Know that you cannot fail; that what you most certainly expect, that is the thing you will have.

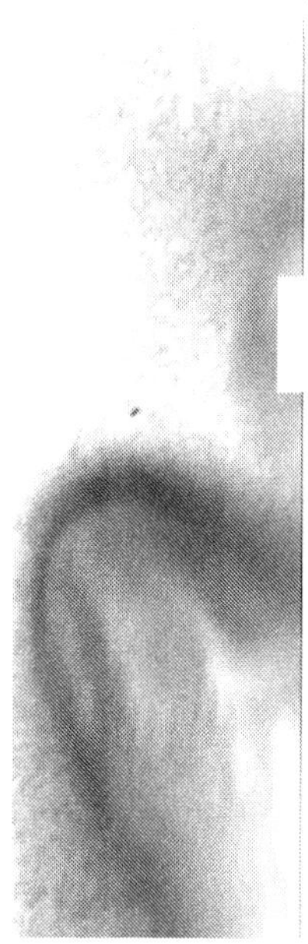

www.ingramcontent.com/pod-product-compliance
Ingram Content Group UK Ltd.
Pitfield, Milton Keynes, MK11 3LW, UK
UKHW020730250326
11478UKWH00033B/438

9 781022 783652